INVESTING FOR

HOW TO BE AN INTELLIGENT INVESTOR AND MAKE MONEY ON ANY MARKET

Descrierea CIP a Bibliotecii Naționale a României

Investing for Beginners. How To Be An Intelligent Investor
And Make Money On Any Market. – Bucharest: My Ebook
Publishing House, 2018
    ISBN 978-606-983-625-5

INVESTING FOR BEGINNERS

HOW TO BE AN INTELLIGENT INVESTOR AND MAKE MONEY ON ANY MARKET

My Ebook Publishing House
Bucharest, 2018

INTRODUCTION

I want to thank you and congratulate you for downloading the book, *"Investing for Beginners: How To Be An Intelligent Investor And Make Money On Any Market"*

This book contains proven steps and strategies on how to take advantage of investment opportunities that abound. It will guide you on the proper approach needed to achieve success in all your future investments.

Thanks again for downloading this book, I hope you enjoy it!

CONTENTS

Chapter 1

INCREASING YOUR INVESTMENT POTENTIALS

We all want the good things of life but are finding it quite hard in picking the right platform for improvement in our finances. If you wish for such enhancements then why sit around and wait for your desires to be met by an "unforeseen hand." Why don't you take the initiative, **Why not Invest?**

Investments create avenues to increase your finances or just put they build and preserve wealth. You must be ready to part away with your money to gain some more, without doing so, do not expect improvements. Investments increase your financial potentials; they give you returns.

Savings versus Investing

Savings refers to deposit money to be used in buying clothes or buying a car or whatever shortly. Investment mainly involves using your money to make more money to achieve a long-term goal. Savings can sometimes incur interest, but this is only applicable to short-term goals. If you wish to stash up for retirement or buy a home, then such savings will not help you in any way.

It is important to understand that you can only invest what you saved up. Savings are the starting point of investment. You must not borrow funds to invest; your personal funds are the best input on any investment. Why? Because if you spend your own savings, then you become the sole receptor of your achievements.

How do I save to invest?

A lot of us have serious money management issues, we spend as we earn, in fact, we spend more than what we make. We are deep in debt. These debts we incurred are actually a product of our erroneous lifestyle.

Financial problems arise from your lifestyle; there are frequent mistakes you make unconsciously every day that gear you up towards failure they include:

1. *Not planning:* It is the nature of humans to procrastinate. We enjoy an

extension of deadlines. We readily allow our debts to accumulate over a period of time.

2. *Overspending*: We spend more than we have. We desire the best out of life, and so we live above our means.

3. *Delaying saving for retirements*: Most people do not access their future; they do not think or make plans about how their 60th birthday will be celebrated. They have no savings for that period in life when activities of youthfulness have become nonexistent,

4. *Fall prey to the financial sales pitch*: A lot of people immediately invest in things they have no knowledge about, they fall victim to the juicy words of a salesman. You must stay clear of the people who pressure you into making quick decisions; they usually have a lot of hidden charges.

5. *Not having extensive knowledge in the investment areas*: Some people invest in individual businesses just because their friends invested in it. They have no prior experience of the subject matter. They do not know about the rules of engagement; they fall prey for the "in vogue" concept, that is, they make decisions based on what everyone else is doing.

6. *Making decisions based on emotions:* A lot of us are vulnerable to our feelings especially those associated with fear and greed that we make financial decisions based on them.

All these are mistakes associated with our daily lives that point on towards failures. These mistakes are made because of our lifestyle preferences. It is essential to change your lifestyle patterns if you wish you save up for investments. You must limit certain parts of your lifestyle if you want to get high up the economic ladder. Some of the things you need get rid off include:

- Smoking
- Alcohol
- Partying
- Gambling
- Unwarranted vacations
- Excessive eating habits
- Laziness towards taking the initiative.

Once you can eliminate or control these activities, your savings will improve and so will your investment potentials.

Yes, it is probably not easy, but you must develop the mindset that it is only by investing in the right lifestyle that you achieve financial success. You must set your mind to the price and prepare for the journey ahead. You must take the initiative and put away does dimes to build up your investment portfolio.

Chapter 2

UNDERSTANDING THE CONCEPT OF INVESTMENT

An Investment is an asset or item purchased with the sole aim of gaining profit shortly. A lot of us have heard about investments. We have even at one time in life made a few "investments" but are clueless about the laws that govern the world of investment and so due to our limited knowledge of the concept of investment, we earn liabilities and not wealth.

You have to understand the rules of investing, its pitfalls and every knowledge involved before you invest. Without having this knowledge, all one's efforts will only meet with failure. You cannot buy stocks just because your friends are buying shares. You cannot make an investment in a specific business only because it looks profitable. You must evaluate, analyze and expand on the principles of finance. If you fail to do so then it would have been better, you did not venture into it since your efforts only but a waste.

Why Invest?

Before investing, you must be able to answer this question:

What is my personal reason for investing in this venture?

Am I seeking financial security?

Am I willing to part with my money for this long?

What do I need to do to bring about the success of this business?

Simply put:

You must plan and define your goals before taking the leap.

Planning is a systematic and careful evaluation of the task ahead. This means you must consider everything about your investment before investing.

This means that you must understand the three central concepts that cover the field of investing. That is, you must:

1. Define your goals and investment time frame

2, You must understand asset allocation

3. You must look after your investment.

Defining your Investment goals

To succeed at anything, you must have a purpose set in stone only dynamic to specific circumstances. You must be able to determine the time frame of your investment and the reasons for your investment. It is essential that you be profoundly realistic when picking up an investment opportunity. Whether it is building on financial security, getting rich, building your retirement funds or merely increasing your income, it's good to have a clear picture of what you really want so that you venture into the part that suits your style.

Naturally, Time frame is very crucial to your investment portfolio. The longer your investments, the more the returns, this is very true to all investments plans.

Picture this #. You have got a savings account; it incurs interest over time, the more the money stays in the account, the more money you make.

Growth asset

These are designed to provide returns in the way of capital growth over a given period of time. They may inform of equity or property investments such as investing in a business venture, investing in real estate, etc. These sort of long-term investments usually protect against inflation.'

The most important feature of this type of investment is that it is done over an extended period of time.They have the potential of producing higher proceeds over the long term.

Income assets

There are kinds of investments usually generate returns over in both long and short periods of time. These returns are generally in the form of cash, bonds, and individual equities. The advantage income assets have overgrowth assets that it tends to be more stable, but it is a disadvantage as it brings forth lower returns.

This gives a better picture of what the types of investments can do for you, its benefits and flaws.

Chapter 3

EMOTIONAL GUIDE TO FINANCIAL INVESTMENTS

Our Emotions are double-edged swords. They can make you a success or a failure. A favorite behavioral economist, Thaler stated once in an economic theory on idealized conception of behavior, "bestowing on humans the mind of a computer and the willpower of a saint, if this were possible, then people will rationally calculate how much they need to retire, save and invest, then reduce their consumptions accordingly, invest optimally, never splurge or speculate".

This theory is very correct, were we like computers, we will never make irrational decisions. We will not be subject to the ups and downs of our emotions. We will not be subject to our fears, unruly desires, greed, etc. We will only make decisions based on facts and facts alone. But since it is impossible to make decisions based on only rational thinking, it is important we understand how to maximize our emotions to our better good.

Reflecting money through our emotions

It is quite natural that when we talk of money, we speak excitedly only about closed deals, bargains or winnings. We do not talk about debts or loans or impoverishment.

We all value and desire to have money and lots of it, but when we look around, all we see is that the average man deep in debt, living below the accepted standard of living and "dreaming big."

Yes, we all know about money, but only a few of us truly understand the true essence of money.

Money is a symbol used in exchange for goods and service; a means to convene all commitments and assess the value of something. We are driven by our want for money that we most times do not consider the essence of it. We only value what it can provide for us at that moment.

Our love for the things Money can give us is usually bordered by Pride, regret, speculations, peer influence, risk, etc.

We usually do not follow the accepted rules of money; we only let our decisions be clouded by our prejudice towards the above factors.

To advance and enjoy the joys of quality decisions it is good we understand this bias and curb our responsibility towards them. It is imperative we manage our emotions efficiently and enhance our financial status.

It is a terrible misconception to say that Emotions are awful. Emotions are what make us humans; they are our unique quality. Feelings are important in validating every logical reasoning. They filter and reaffirm our decisions. This strongly infers that we do need to learn the necessary strategies to be able to use our Emotions alongside logic to enhance our financial matters.

The only thing is to tone the right emotions into place. Not all emotions we feel can help us out in matters such as investment. For example, Fear is probably not the best factor. It can cripple your investing capacity (ability to let go of your money at the right time) You have to develop the right mindset.

What is the Investors Mindset?

When it comes to investing, the poor and the average usually choose to do nothing or venture into this territory. The poor and the standard prefer to save only in their bank accounts. They want the extra income that can be acquired from investments but never do anything about it.

Their financial strategy involves "I will not take any risk, I do not want to lose" this is a very poor mindset. To excel at your investments, you must develop the right mindset. You must let go of your fears and calculate or risks logically to your advantage.

All investments have a risk factor. The difference is in your ability to logically calculate and evaluate.

Naturally, the experience can give almost the best teaching on how and what to do about investments but this is a costly method and probably not a specific manner.

So, to become equally very good at finances, it is critical that you gain financial intelligence. This is the only way to sort things through. Financial decisions made by looking at facts, interpreting and evaluation information and estimating all anticipated risks are the best method s of making money. This, in turn, gets embedded in our brains, it slowly becomes art, and at some points, we begin to make the most positive decisions unconsciously due to the better financial habits we have held on to over the years.

Hence to add to the previous list of things you should do before investing, we have:

You must gain necessary financial intelligence, and you must seek the help of Financial Advisors.

Chapter 3

RISK MANAGEMENT

There is no such thing as an investment without risks. We are often misled with some claims that specific packages are risk-free. It is crucial that this phenomenon is understood accurately.

A Risk is any form of circumstance; seen or unseen that can bring about negative results. There are several different types of risks, they include:

Inflation risks

Inflation measures the rate of increase in general prices for goods and services precisely. Inflation can disintegrate the value or the purchasing power of your investments

Currency risk

This risk is associated with the exchange rates of your currency. It can make the value of your investment to decline.

Country risk

This risk is associate events that affect your country. It could be war, political crisis, natural disasters or financial problems causing weakness in your country's financial market.

Liquidity risk

This involves the ability of your investment to make a profit, that is, it is the measure of how difficult your investment can be sold or bought.

Market risk

This type of risk is prevalent among almost all types of investments. They are concerned with the fluctuations that can arise in the financial market that can affect your investment returns.

Shortfall risk

This type of risk is associated with the ability of your investments to meet your long-term financial goals, that is, the ability of there continuous growth and not depreciation in value.

How do you minimize risk?

First of all, it is important you note that there is no such thing as a risk-free investment. The best easy to minimize risk is to diversify your investments, that is, spread your money across different investments. These reduce risks associated with sudden fall in the financial market or individual investment market.

You should also note that it is not possible to have a risk free business portfolio. In fact, diversification doesn't also ensure that you get to profit from your investments, but it can help you reduce the impact of losing all at once. Diversification only brings in an avenue of the fact that even if some of your investments are declining, the others can help you through such down moments.

Chapter 5

THE IMPORTANCE OF COST AND TAX

The cost in this context refers to the amount spent outside of the real money placed on your investments. It relates to administrative fees, fees paid to your financial advisor, etc.

They are incurred by the way and manner with which you organize your investments. They depend on your method of investment.

Investing directly

This type of investment may only incur charges or administrative fees as will be listed below. For instance, if you decide to invest in bonds, you will need to pay broker's fees on watch transactions which can vary and by so doing depends on the type of broker you decided to use.

Investing through a financial advisor

It is usually best to invest through a financial advisor since he knows the pros and cons of the market. He can help you minimize certain costs, as he knows which ones are better, he has intimate knowledge of the types of brokers that exist and so on. But take note, your financial adviser will also charge you a fee. So weigh your options carefully, there are markets you can infiltrate without going this far.

Types of Cost:

There are so many charges that can be incurred when making an investment of which we cannot go through all of them. We can only take a look at some of them.

Initial charge: this is the charge placed on the investment by the fund manager(the owner or manager of the investment). It is usually a percentage of your initial investment

Exit fee or redemption fee: some fund managers place a charge and generally return the proceeds to the fund to cover securities and by so doing protect other existing investors after you have pulled out.

Annual Management Charge (AMC): this is the fee paid to the Fund manager for managing the investment

Stamp Duty Tax: This is to be paid to the Revenue and customs service in different countries.

Ongoing charge Figure (OCF): These charges cover administration, audit, legal, registration, etc. concerning the type of funds invested in. These charges are paid periodically.

Tax

It is crucial you understand how the tax system works to enhance your investment returns. There are different types of charge, some of the can be avoided, some cannot be avoided. A tax such as Stamp Duty cannot be avoided.   Different types of Tax exist with the various investment types. Your Investment type will affect the level and type of tax you will pay. Based on Tax efficiency investments are divided into two: Individual Savings account and Capital Gains Tax

Individual Savings account (ISA)

These types of investments include investing in things such as Stocks and bonds. They are usually taxed efficiently as they allow you to save and invest a limited amount. All incomes earned and gains you make on the funds held within this are free of tax

Capital Gains Tax (CGT)

This type of Tax is charged on the sale of an individual's possession which exceeds a set amount each year. There are some exceptions to this tax; they include this such as Savings and Investment bonds, ISAs, etc.

Chapter 6

TYPES OF INVESTMENTS
(ASSET ALLOCATION)

Asset allocation refers merely to the way and manner in which you spread your investments to suit your objectives, time frame, and risk potentials.

There are different types of Assets, and they have different time frames, objectives and types of risks associated with them. It is important you understand all of them before choosing which of them to choose.

Equities

Equities represent the value of ownership of a given business. They provide the right to have returned from the success of s business entity. They can be in the form of stocks or shares. Equities have the highest potential to bring profits over a long term. They depend on the success of the business. It is a misconception if you feel that Equities come without risks. If the said business, you invested in runs into trouble, then it is possible to lose all your investments. You must note that the value of your investments may rise or fall.

Usually, you are required to pay dividends to the company you invested in; this is dependent on the company's earnings and management strategy.

Bonds

A bond is a loan which can be made to a company, government, etc. That is, it is the amount of money you loaned a company or government or an institution. This money will incur interest rates over time. They are different from equity in the sense that you have no rights and ownership of the said institution, all you receive is your interest. They help offset the instability of equities invested in. They are issued for a period of time a and are opposite regarding rising and fall with equity. Bonds typically offer regular payments and have a fixed amount of interest.

Bonds are dependent on the type of institution that issues it. For instance, the types of bonds issued by a company are called corporate bonds while the forms issued by the government have different names. In the Uk, it is called gits.

Property

This is one of the most accepted ways of investment especially in the areas of real estate in the way of getting home. Real Estate takes a whole lot more funds to invest in the real estate, but you can make more profits from these investments. You can make money by buying an estate and then leasing it out to others for periodic payments. There is always a market for this type of investment; people are always looking for apartments to lease temporarily. You can take the initiative.

Cash Investments

These types of investments include investments placed in the banks or co-operative societies which incur an interest rate over time. They offer one crucial factor, ability to withdraw cash quite quickly. Cash investments are least volatile, but they give the lowest of returns. They are better used as emergency funds and funds that can be used for short-term objectives.

Other Kinds of investments:

Gold: Gold may be an outdated form of investment, but it comes with minimal risk. By Gold, I don't mean only investing in jewelry but also investing in coins or bullion bars. The good thing about Gold is that it is not affected by inflation and cannot be reduced by economic trends. They only appreciate, there is no such thing as depreciation with Gold.

Peer to Peer Lending: You can start a sort of cooperative society within your locality, where people come to you for loans to carry out their businesses and you receive a set amount of interest periodically. To minimize the risk of losing your money if the said individual becomes bankrupt, it is advisable that you do not loan all your funds to one party but spread them across different individuals.

Chapter 7

MANAGING YOUR INVESTMENTS

There are different ways with which one can achieve his/her finances, but the best and easiest way is by use of pooled funds.

Pooled funds refer to a fund that is brought together by two or more investors into one single investment account. These groups can be investment clubs, partnerships or trusts. The idea is to invest in stocks, bonds, etc. together mutually. What they do is get the services of a Fund manager to analyze the investments accurately and watch over it.

Advantages of Pooled funds	Disadvantages of Pooled funds
Diversification: this reduces the risk of losing a whole lot on a single investment	Since input in a particular investment is small. Then significant gain from it is not possible
Professional Management: Fund managers usually have extensive research on the market	Pooled funds do not speak for your objectives. They are only subject to the purposes of the Fund manager
Liquidity: You can have access to your money at any time as shares can be bought and sold at any time	There are no guarantees as the value can fluctuate at any time. Especially if your set shares are less than what you paid for them

Types of Pooled funds

Unit trust: This type of pooled fund is placed under the trust, meaning the manager has exclusive right to create or cancel units at any time depending on public demand.

Open-Ended Investment Company (OEIC): in this type of pooled funds, the units are called shares but are governed by a Law, they cannot be traded on a stock exchange only by the company, and the company issues shares depending on the number of buyers and sellers.

Investment trust: this is a closed-end fund meaning there is a limited number of shares as established by the Company with the aim of producing returns by investing in other companies. They trade like stock exchanges and can be purchased at any time. They can also be sold through a Stockbroker.

Exchange Traded Funds (ETFs): These refer to any type of asset that can be traded on a stock market. They may be shares or bonds depending on the company, and they constitute a significant proportion of any financial market.

How do you manage your Investments?

The assets you invest in will rise or fall over time as markets are infused by the happenings in the financial market. It is also influenced by the economic, social and political trends of the given period. You must always remember that market sometimes fluctuate slowly and other times more dramatically.

This means that you should not lose sight of your goals and aspirations when investing and try as hard as possible not to change investments directly because it fluctuated dramatically. You have to weigh all the odds; your financial adviser is also needed when you are contemplating this move. They may give you objective advice as against your already emotional one.

You should also understand that there is no such thing as timing the market. Trying hard to pick such best times means you have no plans to invest or make substantial gains at all. Even financial managers cannot adequately predict and comprehend the market at all times.

You must review your investments from time to time depending not only on the market but on all changes in your personal situation. During this review, you may decide to change investments or rebalance then by either topping up, transferring or reinvesting dividends. Remember to weigh all options tactfully and logically.

Start Investing?

After perfect understanding of everything about investments, you can set right to investing your funds in your desired manner. It's always good to seek the services of a Financial adviser before doing so as you'll be equipped with the precise view of the market, you wish to invest into.

You must always note that successful investments only arise from knowing your desires, understanding the time frame factor for any investment and indicating your attitude towards its risk factor and then make a plan based on your own objectives.

Remember to review regularly and also importantly keep an eye on your costs and Tax.

CONCLUSION

Thank you again for downloading this book!

I hope this book was able to help you with your investment choices and enhance your success rate in this new venture.

The Next step is to take the initiative and start investing. Remember the journey doesn't begin until there is a step in that direction.

Finally, if you enjoyed this book, then I'd like to ask you for a favor, would you be kind enough to leave a review for this book? It'd be much appreciated!

Thank you and good luck!

www.ingramcontent.com/pod-product-compliance
Lightning Source LLC
Chambersburg PA
CBHW071125210326
41519CB00020B/6419